THE
RADICAL
QUESTION

DAVID
PLATT

MULTNOMAH
BOOKS

THE RADICAL QUESTION
PUBLISHED BY MULTNOMAH BOOKS
12265 Oracle Boulevard, Suite 200
Colorado Springs, Colorado 80921

Scripture quotations are taken from the Holy Bible, New International Version®. NIV®. Copyright © 1973, 1978, 1984 by International Bible Society. Used by permission of Zondervan Publishing House. All rights reserved.

Details in some anecdotes and stories have been changed to protect the identities of the persons involved.

ISBN 978-1-60142-321-4

Portions of this booklet have been adapted from *Radical*, copyright © 2010 by David Platt, published by Multnomah Books.

Published in association with Yates & Yates, LLP, Attorneys and Counselors, Orange, California.

Published in the United States by WaterBrook Multnomah, an imprint of the Crown Publishing Group, a division of Random House Inc., New York.

MULTNOMAH and its mountain colophon are registered trademarks of Random House Inc.

Printed in the United States of America
2010

10 9 8 7 6 5 4

SPECIAL SALES
Most WaterBrook Multnomah books are available at special quantity discounts when purchased in bulk by corporations, organizations, and special-interest groups. Custom imprinting or excerpting can also be done to fit special needs. For information, please e-mail SpecialMarkets@WaterBrook Multnomah.com or call 1-800-603-7051.

THE
RADICAL
QUESTION

Imagine a scene that took place in Asia not long ago:

A room in an ordinary house, dimly lit, all the blinds on the windows closed. Twenty leaders from churches in the region sit quietly in a circle on the floor, their Bibles open. They speak in hushed tones or not at all. Some still glisten with sweat; others' clothes and shoes are noticeably dusty. They have been walking or riding bicycles since early morning when they left distant villages to get here.

Whenever a knock is heard or a suspicious sound drifts in, everyone freezes while a burly, tough-looking man gets up to check things out.

These men and women have gathered in secret, arriving intentionally at different times throughout the day so as not to draw attention. In this country it is illegal for Christians to come together like this. If caught, the people here could lose their land, their jobs, their families, even their lives...

■ ■ ■

I was in that dimly lit room that day, a visitor from America. I huddled next to an interpreter, who helped me understand their stories as they began to share.

The tough-looking man—our "head of security"—was the first to speak up. But as he spoke, his intimidating appearance quickly gave way to reveal a tender heart.

"Some of the people in my church have been pulled away by a cult," he said. Tears welled up in his eyes. "We are hurting. I need

God's grace to lead my church through these attacks."

The cult that had been preying on his church is known for kidnapping Christians, taking them to isolated locations, and torturing them, my interpreter explained. Many brothers and sisters in the area would never tell the good news again. At least not with words. Their tongues had been cut out.

■ *The tough-looking man*
■ *was the first to speak up.*

A woman on the other side of the room spoke next. "Some of the members in my church were recently confronted by government officials," she said. "They threatened their families, saying that if they did not stop gathering to study the Bible, they were going to lose everything they had." She asked for prayer, then said, "I need to know how to lead my church to follow Christ even when it costs them everything."

I looked around the room. Now everyone was in tears. They looked at one another, then several said at once, "We need to pray."

Immediately they went to their knees, and with their faces on the floor, they began to cry out with muted intensity to God. Their praying was not marked by lofty language but by heartfelt praise and pleading.

"O God, thank you for loving us!"

"O God, we need you!"

"Jesus, we trust in you!"

"Jesus, you are worthy!"

One after another they prayed while others wept.

After about an hour the room grew silent, and the men and women rose from the floor.

All around the room, on the floor where each had prayed, I saw puddles of tears.

■ ■ ■

The brothers and sisters in that Asian country have shown by their sacrifices just how much Jesus is worth to them. He is worth *everything* to them.

And they are not alone.

They are joined by brothers and sisters in Sudan who believe Jesus is worthy of their trust, even amid pain and persecution of genocidal proportions.

They are joined by brothers and sisters in India who believe Jesus is worthy of their devotion, even when they face threats from Muslim extremists in the north and Hindu extremists in the south.

They are joined by brothers and sisters all

over the Middle East who believe Jesus is worthy of their love, even when their family members threaten to kill them for professing belief in him.

They are joined by brothers and sisters around the world who believe Jesus is worthy of all their hopes, all their dreams, all their desires, all their possessions, all their plans, and all their lives.

But are they joined by you and me?

A DIFFERENT SCENE

Three weeks after traveling to underground house churches in Asia, I began my first Sunday as the pastor of a church in America. The scene was much different. No dimly lit rooms here; we were occupying an auditorium with theater-style lighting. Instead of traveling for miles by foot or bicycle to gather for worship, we had all arrived in millions of dollars' worth of vehicles. Dressed in our fine clothes, we sat in cushioned chairs.

To be honest, there was not much at stake. Many had come because this was their normal routine. Some had come simply to check out the new pastor. I don't think any had come at the risk of their lives.

> *In America, the scene was much different. We had all arrived in millions of dollars' worth of vehicles.*

That afternoon crowds filled the parking lot of our sprawling multimillion-dollar church campus for a celebration. Moms, dads, and their kids jumped around together on inflatable games brought in for the occasion. Church members discussed a plan for using the adjacent open land to build state-of-the-art recreation fields and facilities to support more events like this. Everyone, it seemed, looked forward to a successful future.

Please don't misunderstand this scene I'm describing. It was filled with wonderful, Bible-believing Christians who genuinely wanted to welcome me and enjoy one another. People like you and me—people who desire community, who want to be involved in church, and who believe God is important in their lives. But as a new pastor comparing the images around me that day with the pictures, still fresh in my mind, of brothers and sisters on the other side of the world, I could not help but think that somewhere along the way we in America have lost touch with what is essential, radical—even dangerous— about our faith and replaced it with what is comfortable.

In the days that followed, I began looking further at my own life, at the church God has entrusted to me to pastor, and at the church culture around me. As I did, I was overwhelmed by the differences between our version of Christianity and the version of Christianity that prevails among our brothers and sisters around the world.

Instead of weeping together on our faces before God, we calmly sit on plush chairs in beautiful buildings.

Instead of going against the grain in our culture, we settle into our culture with lifestyles that are virtually indistinguishable from the world around us.

Instead of a simple, costly, humble, authentic, passionate, risky pursuit of Christ, we prioritize clean, elaborate, entertaining, slick, innovative church programs and performances that cater to our personal tastes.

And in light of these differences, I am

convinced we need to answer a fundamentally important question. What is Jesus worth to us?

REDEFINING JESUS

Do we believe that Jesus is worthy of sacrifice in our lives? Our immediate thought would probably be, *Yes. Sure. Of course.*

But listen to how we describe what it means to follow him.

Ask Jesus to come into your heart.

Invite Jesus to come into your life.

Pray this prayer, sign this card, or walk down this aisle, and accept Jesus as your personal Savior.

You will not find one of these casual, contemporary catch phrases in Scripture. Instead, in Jesus' mouth you will find words that are foreign to us today. You will find phrases that show us he is worthy of far more than a polite invitation. He is worthy of supreme devotion. Let me give you a few examples.

At the end of Luke 9, we find the stories of three men who approach Jesus, eager to follow him. Surprisingly, in each case Jesus seems to try to talk them *out* of doing so!

The first guy says, "I will follow you wherever you go."

Jesus responds, "Foxes have holes and birds of the air have nests, but the Son of Man has no place to lay his head."[1] In other words, Jesus tells this man that he can expect homelessness on the journey ahead. Even when the basic need of shelter is not guaranteed, Jesus is worthy of all our trust.

The second man tells Jesus that his father has just died. The man wants to go back, bury his father, and then follow Jesus.

Jesus replies, "Let the dead bury their own dead, but you go and proclaim the kingdom of God."[2]

What could he mean by that?

> ■ *I remember the moment I*
> ■ *learned that my own dad*
> ■ *had died of a heart attack.*

I remember distinctly the moment I learned that my own dad had died of a heart attack. In the days that followed, my heart was filled with an immense heaviness and a deep desire to honor my dad at his funeral. I cannot imagine hearing at that point these words from Jesus: "Don't even go to your dad's funeral. There are more important things to do." Yet that's the essence of what Jesus tells the second man who comes up to him. Jesus is worthy of total allegiance and immediate obedience.

A third man approaches Jesus and tells him that he wants to follow him, but before he does, he needs to say good-bye to his family.

Makes sense. But Jesus tells the man, "No one who puts his hand to the plow and looks back is fit for service in the kingdom of God."[3] Plainly put, a relationship with Jesus requires absolute, undivided, exclusive affection.

Trust me, even if it means becoming homeless.

Follow me, even if it means letting someone else bury your dad.

Love me, even if it means not saying good-bye to your family.

Jesus is worthy of radical devotion.

The first time I heard this text from Luke 9 preached, it was from the lips of Dr. Jim Shaddix. He was my preaching professor, and I had moved to New Orleans specifically to study under him. Soon after I got there, Dr. Shaddix invited me to travel with him to an event where he was speaking. I sat in the front row in a crowd of hundreds of people, and I listened as he began to speak.

"Tonight my goal is to talk you out of following Jesus."

My eyebrows shot up in amazement and confusion. What was he thinking? What was *I* thinking? My wife and I had moved to New Orleans to study under a guy who persuades people *not* to follow Jesus?

Dr. Shaddix preached the sermon exactly as Luke 9 describes, warning potential disciples about what is involved in following Jesus. At the end he invited people who wanted to follow Christ to come down to the front. To my surprise, many in the crowd got up from their seats and came down.

I sat there dumbfounded. Then insight struck. *So this is just a preaching tactic, kind of a sanctified reverse psychology. And it works. Tell*

*them you're going to talk them out of following
Jesus, and they will respond in droves.*

I decided I was going to try it.

> ■ *My eyebrows shot up in*
> ■ *amazement and confusion.*
> ■ *What was he thinking?*
> ■ *What was I thinking?*

The next week I was preaching at a youth
event. Taking my cue from Dr. Shaddix, I
proudly stood before the students assembled
that night and announced, "My goal tonight
is to talk you out of following Jesus." I could
see the leaders of the event raise their eyebrows
in concern, but I knew what I was doing. After
all, I'd been in seminary for a few weeks, and
I'd seen this done before. So I preached the
message and then invited students who wanted
to follow Christ to come forward.

Apparently I was more successful than Dr. Shaddix in preaching that message. Let's just say that I stood alone at the front until the event organizer finally decided it was time for me to call it a night. For some reason I was never invited back.

Unlike what I thought about Dr. Shaddix, Jesus was not pulling a gimmick in order to get more followers. On the contrary, Jesus often seemed totally unwilling to cater to the crowds. He is so unlike us. We will do whatever it takes to draw the masses, but Jesus was constantly turning them away. Whenever the crowd would get big, he'd say something like, "Unless you eat the flesh of the Son of Man and drink his blood, you have no life in you."[4] Not exactly the sharpest church-growth tactic. I can picture the look on the disciples' faces. I can imagine their minds racing. *No, not the drink-my-blood speech! We'll never make*

the list of fastest-growing movements if you keep
asking them to eat you!

> **Can you imagine your church**
> **deciding to stream those words**
> **across its home page for every**
> **new visitor to see? Jesus just**
> **lost most of us at hello.**

On another occasion when Jesus was sur-
rounded by a throng of eager followers, he
turned to them and remarked, "If anyone
comes to me and does not hate his father and
mother, his wife and children, his brothers
and sisters—yes, even his own life—he cannot
be my disciple."[5] Can you imagine your
church deciding to stream those words across
its home page for every new visitor to see?
Jesus just lost most of us at hello.

But Jesus had more to say: "Anyone who

does not carry his cross and follow me cannot be my disciple."[6]

Now this is taking it to another level. *Pick up an instrument of torture and follow me.* This is getting weird…and kind of creepy. Imagine a leader coming on the scene today and inviting all who would come after him to pick up an electric chair and become his disciples. Any takers?

As if this were not enough, Jesus rounded out his seeker-sensitive plea with a pull-at-your-heartstrings conclusion. "Any of you who does not give up everything he has cannot be my disciple."[7] Give up everything you have, carry a cross, and hate your family. You have to agree, this sounds a lot different than "Admit, believe, confess, and pray a prayer after me."

Yet one more potential disciple approached Jesus and asked what he needed to do in order to be a part of Christ's kingdom. This eager seeker was young, rich, intelligent, and influential—a prime prospect for any growing movement.

But what was Jesus' reply? "Sell everything you have and give to the poor.... Then come, follow me."[8]

The man turned away, persuaded that the cost was too high.

Let's put ourselves in the shoes of these followers of Jesus in the first century. What if you were the man Jesus told not to even say good-bye to his family? What if we were told to hate our families and give up everything we had in order to follow Jesus? What if we were told to sell all our possessions in order to give to the poor?

This is where we come face to face with a dangerous reality. We *do* have to give up everything we have to follow Jesus. We *do*

have to love him in a way that makes our closest relationships in this world look like hate.
And it is entirely possible that he *will* tell any
one of us to sell everything we have and give
it to the poor.

But we don't want to believe it.

> - *We take the Jesus of the Bible*
> - *and begin twisting him into*
> - *a version of Jesus that we are*
> - *more comfortable with.*

We are afraid of what this might mean for
our lives. So we rationalize these passages away.
"Jesus wouldn't really tell us not to bury our
father or not to say good-bye to our family.
Jesus didn't literally mean to sell all we have
and give it to the poor. What Jesus really
meant was…"

And this is where we need to pause. We

need to pause because we are redefining Christianity according to our preferences. We are giving in to the dangerous temptation to take the Jesus of the Bible and begin twisting him into a version of Jesus that we are more comfortable with.

A nice, middle-class, American Jesus.

A Jesus who doesn't mind material security and would never call us to give away everything we have.

A Jesus who would not expect us to forsake our closest relationships so that he receives all our affection.

A Jesus who wants us to be balanced, who wants us to avoid dangerous extremes, who for that matter wants us to avoid danger altogether.

A Jesus who is fine with a devotion from us that does not infringe on our comforts, because after all he loves us just the way we are.

But do you and I realize what we are doing at this point? We are molding Jesus into our image and making him look like us. And the danger now is that when we gather to sing and lift our hands in worship, we are not actually worshiping the Jesus of the Bible. Instead, we are worshiping ourselves.

Meanwhile, the Jesus of the Bible is supremely worthy of sacrificial devotion. His portrait in Scripture evokes immediate and total submission. He is the Alpha and Omega, the Beginning and the End, the First and the Last, the Final Amen. He is the Bread of Life, Christ our Creator, our Deliverer, our Everlasting Father—he is God. He is the Good Shepherd, the Great High Priest, the Holy One, the image of the invisible God. He is King of kings and Lord of lords, majestic and mighty, and no one compares to him, the only begotten Son of the Father, full of grace and truth. He is the power of God, the Resurrection and the Life, the Supreme Sacrifice, the Way, the Truth, and the Life, the very Word of God made flesh.

When we see a biblical picture of Jesus, we realize that the greatness of who he is demands the surrender of all we are and have.

A New American Dream

Yet we are tempted to give him less than he deserves. Instead of radical devotion to Christ, we so easily settle for nominal devotion to him while we indulge ourselves in other pursuits. We are captivated by an American dream. Told at every turn to believe in ourselves, trust in ourselves, and promote ourselves, we work to gain it all: a comfortable life, a good career, a decent family, and an easy retirement. Sure, we tack church attendance onto the end of everything, but at the core our lives are consumed with a dream of success, security, safety, and satisfaction in all this world has to offer.

> ■ *What if Jesus is worthy*
> ■ *of more in our lives than*
> ■ *a Christian spin on the*
> ■ *American dream?*

But what if there is another way? What if we were created for a much greater purpose? What if we were created, not to advance ourselves, but to deny ourselves? What if Jesus is worthy of more in our lives than a Christian spin on the American dream? And what if there is greater, more lasting success, security, safety, and satisfaction that can be found only in radical devotion to him?

Imagine the American dream in action.

Imagine a university student preparing for

his profession. All his life he has been told to work hard at school so he can go to college, get a degree, and build a career. With the right amount of motivation, dedication, and intuition, he can make something of himself one day. So he presses on toward that goal.

Or imagine a gifted businessman who has reached his aspirations. He started with humble roots and faced daunting challenges, but he persevered through long days at the office and short nights at home to get to the top. He arrived there faster than he expected, and though it was not always easy, in the end he believes it was worth it. He now lives in an expansive suburban home with his wife and children, a self-made man with all he needs.

And then there is the married couple beginning retirement. Finally the wait is over, and the options abound. Settle into a quiet, secluded home, or travel across the country?

Renovate the house, or take out a second mortgage on one in the mountains? Buy a fishing boat, or take up golf lessons? The pleasures they now enjoy are a monument to the years of labor that have made it all possible.

> *Imagine these common scenarios, and then ask the question, "What if we were created for something much greater than this?"*

Imagine these common scenarios, and then ask the question, "What if we were created for something much greater than this?"

Let me introduce you to Daniel, a college student like the one I mentioned earlier. He is a member of our faith family and recently graduated with honors from a nearby university with a degree in mechanical engineering.

Coming out of school, he was given two attractive offers: take an extremely high-paying job at a nuclear power plant, or have all his expenses paid to complete master's and doctorate degrees in engineering.

Taking either one of these offers would certainly not have been bad, but two years ago Daniel came to faith in Christ. The focus of his entire life shifted to using the grace of God in his life to make much of the glory of God in the world. Consequently, he turned down both options before him and instead went to work with an engineering program designed to help impoverished communities in third-world countries.

His dad e-mailed me soon after Daniel made this decision. "Daniel has made a very radical departure from my long-held and traditional value system," he wrote. "I have raised my children with solid Christian values and naturally have expected them to grab the brass ring of opportunity and settle into a productive family life." In the rest of the e-mail, though, his dad described how proud he was that his son had let go of the pursuits of this world in order to "take the gospel to places and peoples unknown to him."

> *Jeff climbed the ladder of success only to realize that success in the kingdom of God involves moving down, not up.*

And God has been faithful to Daniel. I met with him in my office a few weeks ago, and he told me about unprecedented opportunities that God is now giving him from America to Africa to Asia as he pursues a much greater dream than he ever had before.

Or let me introduce you to Jeff, a businessman like the one I mentioned earlier, who climbed the ladder of success only to realize that success in the kingdom of God involves moving down, not up. As a young professional, he scaled the heights of success in our culture in almost every conceivable way. I'll let him tell his story in excerpts from a speech he gave to other executives in his company:

> My career has been a complete whirlwind in ways more successful than I ever anticipated it could be. I am paying more in taxes than I ever expected to make in a full year! I have been incredibly blessed. I was able to bring my wife home from work. Then we purchased our dream home in the exact neighborhood where we always wanted to live. I purchased the BMW; I bought

the big beach house; and we went on great vacations. On top of all this, I was growing a business that I truly loved in an industry that I am passionate about. But somehow something was missing from my life, and I couldn't figure out what it was. I have been a Christian since I was seven years old, but through my pursuit of business and success, I somehow had replaced seeking the Lord with pursuing stuff and success.

Then something happened last year that changed my life. I stood in a city dump in Tegucigalpa, Honduras. I saw men, women, and children who were living in a dump where they scoured for food and shelter. Humbled by the reality of parents raising their kids in a dump, I reached my breaking point when I saw a woman eight

months pregnant walk by me, looking
for food. I couldn't decide which was
worse—the fact that the baby was con-
ceived in a dump or that it was going to
be born there. In the middle of this
scene, God asked me, "What are you
going to do with what I have given
you? How are you going to use your in-
fluence, your leadership, and your resources in the world around you?"

For the first time, Jeff realized that God
had a purpose for his life that was greater than
the pursuit of the next and bigger thing. So
Jeff decided to walk away from the American
dream. He still runs his business and makes a
lot of money but not to make much of himself. He and a couple of other guys in our faith
family have begun a ministry that works with
local churches around the world to provide

clean water in communities where thousands are dying every day of preventable waterborne diseases.

Finally, let me introduce you to Ed and Patty. A few years ago when they got to retirement, they had plenty of options for what to do together. But they chose an uncommon path. This year, between July and October, Ed and Patty were home a total of eleven days. Why? Not because they were vacationing, but because they were doing disaster relief in cities and towns that had experienced flooding in the United States. Then they both went to Nigeria. Then Ed went to Sri Lanka, where he cooked meals for the hungry in the middle of rebel fighting. Patty usually travels with him, but Ed told me she doesn't like sleeping under trucks in the middle of rebel fighting, so she passed on the Sri Lanka trip. Ed told me once, "What else am I going to do with

my retirement? I just want to tell as many
people about the gospel as I can."

> *They have been conquered*
> *by a superior ambition...*
> *and they are not alone.*

If you were to meet Daniel, Jeff, Ed, or
Patty, you wouldn't notice anything extraor-
dinary about them. They are ordinary people
who have achieved varying levels of success in
this world. But all of them have this in common: They believe that they were created for
more than a Christian spin on the American
dream. They believe the purpose of their lives
is deeper than having a nice job, raising a decent family, living a comfortable life, and tack-
ing church attendance onto the end of it.
They believe Jesus has called them to a much
higher plane and given them a much greater

dream. They are Christians who have been conquered by a superior ambition, and they are surrendering every facet of their lives to knowing Jesus and making his worth known in all the world.

■ *Will you join the*
■ *movement?*

And they are not alone. They are joined by wealthy doctors who are selling their homes and giving to the poor or moving overseas, business leaders who are mobilizing their companies to help the hurting, young couples who are moving into the inner city to live out the gospel, and senior adults, stay-at-home moms, college students, and teenagers who are reorienting their lives around radical devotion to Jesus.

They are part of a movement of Chris-

tians in American churches today who are re-
discovering what it means to follow Jesus for
who he is, not for who we have created him
to be. A movement of Christians who have
decided they do not have time to play games
with their lives and in church while billions
around the globe suffer and die without
Christ. A movement of Christians who are
forsaking the priorities and pursuits of this
world so that their lives might count in this
world for the spread of the gospel and the
glory of Christ. A movement of Christians
who have decided that settling for casual,
comfortable, complacent, business-as-usual
Christianity is no longer an option. A movement of Christians who are taking Jesus at his
word and sacrificing everything to declare
Jesus to the world, no matter what it costs
them, because they believe he is worth it.

Will you join the movement?

THE WORLD AS IT IS

Look at the world.

See a world where, over the last few years, more than half a million people have died instantly—in tsunamis in southeast Asia, cyclones in Myanmar, earthquakes in China and Pakistan, or floods in Nepal and Bangladesh—and where most of those half-million people had never once heard the gospel. They are joined today by a billion others who at this moment still have not heard that Christ came to save them from their sins.

See a world where half the population is living on less than two dollars a day while you and I, by contrast, are extremely rich.

See the nation of India, where there are more people living below the poverty line than there are total people in the United States.

See a world where today alone twenty-six

thousand children will die either of starvation
or a preventable disease.

See our dogs and cats eating better than
our brothers and sisters in central Africa.

See a world where last fall, in one week
alone, fifty thousand people died of AIDS,
more than a hundred thousand children died
of hunger-related diseases, thousands of other
children were trafficked around the world for
sexual exploitation, and hundreds were killed
in an earthquake in Pakistan. All in one week.
And yet, during that same week, the greatest
concerns for many of us were how our foot-
ball teams played and how our 401(k) ac-
counts fared.

In addition to all this, see thousands upon
thousands of our brothers and sisters in China
and North Korea and Laos and Saudi Arabia
imprisoned and killed because of their faith
in Christ.

See all these things, and realize that the purpose of our lives is not just to have a comfortable life, a good career, a decent family, and an easy retirement in this world. We were created for so much more than this. Jesus is worthy of so much more than this.

We have a choice. We can settle for casual devotion to Jesus, sitting comfortably in our nice church buildings, where we are insulated and isolated from the inner city and the spiritual lostness of the world. We can give a tip of our hats to the purpose of Christ in the world while we go on designing endless activities that revolve around us. We can retreat into our nice, cozy communities where we can live nice, decent lives while we pretend the starving millions do not exist. We can hide behind our catchy phrases and our easy prayers that dilute the awesome reality of who

Jesus is and what it means to follow him. We can spend our Christian lives sitting comfortably in the nurseries of our churches while drinking spiritual milk.

> *We can hide behind our catchy phrases and our easy prayers. Or we can decide that Jesus is worth more.*

Or we can decide that Jesus is worth more than this.

We can decide that he has created us for a much greater purpose. We can decide to die to ourselves and our dreams and our plans, and we can decide to let our hearts be conquered by a superior ambition. Ultimately, we can decide to sacrifice our lives, our gifts, our skills, our time, our families, and our resources to make the great worth of Christ known amid urgent spiritual and physical needs in all the world.

Here's what I want to say to my brothers and sisters in America: let's sacrifice it all!

For the glory of Christ among a billion people who have not even heard the gospel…

For the sake of men, women, and children who are starving, suffering, and dying every single day…

For the millions in your city and my city who do not know Christ and are headed for a Christless eternity…

For ourselves, for our churches, for our families, for our children who will come behind us…

For all of this and more, let's sacrifice it all!

And when we do, we will discover that Jesus is, indeed, absolutely worthy of all our plans and all our dreams and all our ambitions.

THE COST OF
NONDISCIPLESHIP

We realize, of course, that following Christ for who he is will be costly. To sacrifice everything in radical devotion to Jesus means to surrender our lives, our rights, our ambitions, our plans, our dreams, our families, our relationships, our possessions, our safety, our security, our past, our present, and our future to the absolute lordship of Jesus. It is to relinquish to him our control of the way we think, the way we feel, the way we act, the way we relate, and the way we live. As Dietrich Bonhoeffer wrote in his classic book entitled *The Cost of Discipleship*, "When Christ calls a man, he bids him come and die."

Based on what we have heard from Jesus in the Gospels, we would have to agree that the cost of discipleship is great. But before we let this reality dissuade us from following

Christ wholeheartedly, I want to propose that the cost of nondiscipleship is far greater.

> *The cost of discipleship is great. But I want to propose that the cost of nondiscipleship is far greater.*

When Christians shrink back from self-denying faith and settle into self-indulging faith, the price is high. The cost of nondiscipleship is extremely high for people around the world who don't know Christ. Even the most liberal estimates put the number of Christians at one-third of the world's population. This means that at least 4.5 billion people today are without Christ and are destined for an eternal hell. As long as Christians choose to play games in their churches while they spend their lives fulfilling an American dream, billions in need of the gospel will remain hopelessly in the dark. The cost will be high for the lost if we do not follow Christ radically.

The cost of nondiscipleship is also high for the poor in the world. Consider the price when Christians ignore Jesus' commands to give away their possessions for the sake of the poor and instead choose to spend their resources on larger homes, nicer cars, and more stuff. Consider the cost when these Christians gather in churches and choose to spend millions of dollars on nice buildings to drive up to, cushioned chairs to sit in, and endless programs to enjoy for themselves. Consider the cost for the starving multitudes who sit outside the gate of contemporary Christian affluence.

I remember preparing to take my first trip

to Sudan in 2004. The country was still at war, and the Darfur region in western Sudan had just begun to make headlines. A couple of months before we left, I received a Christian news publication in the mail. The front cover had two headlines side by side. I'm not sure if the editor planned for these particular headlines to be next to each other or if he just missed it in a really big way.

On the left the headline read, "First Baptist Church Celebrates New $23 Million Building." A lengthy article followed, celebrating the church's expensive new sanctuary. It described in detail the building's exquisite marble, intricate design, and beautiful stained glass.

On the right was a much smaller article. The headline for it read, "Baptist Relief Helps Sudanese Refugees." Knowing I was about to go to Sudan, my attention was drawn. As I read the article, it described how 350,000 refugees in western Sudan were dying of malnutrition and might not live to the end of the year. It briefly explained their plight and sufferings. When I got to the end of the article, the last sentence said that Baptists had sent money to help relieve the suffering of the Sudanese. I was excited until I got to the amount.

Now, remember what was on the left: "First Baptist Church Celebrates New $23 Million Building." On the right, the article said, "Baptists have raised $5,000 to send to refugees in western Sudan."

Five thousand dollars.

That is not enough to get a plane into Sudan, much less one drop of water to people who need it.

Twenty-three million dollars for an elaborate sanctuary and five thousand dollars for hundreds of thousands of starving men, women, and children, most of whom were dying apart from faith in Christ.

> **Where have we gone wrong? How did we get to the place where this is tolerable?**

Where have we gone wrong?

How did we get to the place where this is tolerable?

Yes, the cost of nondiscipleship is great. The cost of believers not taking Jesus' worth seriously is vast for those who don't know Christ and devastating for those who are starving and suffering around the world.

But they are not the only ones who pay the cost of nondiscipleship. We pay it as well.

IS HE WORTH IT?

Look at what Jesus says when he tells the rich man to abandon his possessions and give to the poor: "Go, sell everything you have and give to the poor, *and you will have treasure in heaven.*"[9]

If we are not careful, we can misconstrue the radical statements from Jesus in the Gospels and begin to think that he does not want the best for us. But he does. Jesus was not trying to strip this rich man of all his pleasure. Instead he was offering him the satisfaction of eternal treasure. Jesus was saying, "It will be better, not just for the poor, but for you too, when you abandon the stuff you are holding on to."

We see the same thing in Matthew 13. There Jesus tells his disciples, "The kingdom of heaven is like treasure hidden in a field.

When a man found it, he hid it again, and then in his joy went and sold all he had and bought that field."[10]

I love this picture. Imagine walking in a field and stumbling upon a treasure that is more valuable than anything else you could ever work for or find in this life. It is more valuable than all you have now or will ever have in the future.

> *In an instant a plan drops fully formed into your imagination.*

You look around and notice that no one else realizes the treasure is there. In an instant a plan drops fully formed into your imagination. You cover up the treasure quickly and walk away, pretending you haven't seen anything. You go into town and begin to sell all your possessions to have enough to buy that field. People think you're crazy. "What are you doing? What are you thinking?" worried friends and family ask.

"See that field over there?" you tell them. "I'm buying it."

They look at you in disbelief. "That's a ridiculous investment," they say. "Why are you trading away everything you have just for that?"

You respond, "I've got a hunch." And you smile to yourself as you walk away.

You smile because you know. You know that in the end you are not really giving away anything at all. Instead you are gaining. Yes, you are abandoning everything you have, but you are also gaining more than you could ever have in any other way. So with joy—with joy!—you sell your possessions. You sacrifice it all.

Why? Because you have found something worth losing everything for.

This is the picture of Jesus in the Gospels. He is something—someone—worth losing everything for. And if we walk away from the Jesus of the Gospels, then we walk away from eternal riches. The cost of nondiscipleship is profoundly greater for us than the cost of discipleship. For if we cling to the trinkets of this world and reject the radical invitation of Jesus, we will miss out on the infinite treasure of knowing and experiencing him.

This brings us to the crucial question for every professing or potential follower of Jesus. What is Jesus worth to you?

Do you believe he is worth abandoning everything for? Do you really believe Jesus is so good, so satisfying, and so rewarding that you will leave all you own and all you are to find your fullness in him? Do you believe him

enough to obey him and to follow him however and wherever he leads, even when the
crowds in our culture—and maybe in our
churches—turn the other way?

> *Let's stop living as though*
> *we need more possessions,*
> *greater positions, or greater*
> *pleasures in this world.*

Let's trust that Jesus is worthy of radical
devotion. Let's take him at his word when he
says that he is a treasure worth giving everything in this world for. Let's stop living as
though we need more possessions, greater po-
sitions, more plaudits, or greater pleasures in
this world. For that matter, let's stop living as
if this world is even our home. And let's start
living as if we were created for another world,
where a Savior waits for all who have forsaken

this world because they believe in his great worth. Let's start living as though this world has nothing for us because Christ is truly everything to us.

Let's join our brothers and sisters around the world who have joyfully sacrificed the comforts, safety, security, pleasures, and priorities of this world in order to follow Christ. Let's join our brothers and sisters who have decided to spend their lives for his glory in the world. Let's join them in trusting that Jesus is, indeed, someone worth losing everything for.

Let's believe that Jesus is worthy of all our trust—even though we may not always be safe in this world, we will always be secure in his hands.

Let's believe that Jesus is worthy of all our plans—he alone knows what is best for our lives, and we will follow him wherever, however, and whenever he leads.

Let's believe that Jesus is worthy of all our obedience—his word demands total allegiance, so when he speaks, we will respond without question or hesitation.

Let's believe that Jesus is worthy of all our dreams—he has created us for so much more than acclaim in this world, and we will settle for nothing less than his fame in all the world.

Is Jesus worth this to you?

Let's believe that Jesus is worthy of all our possessions—he has given them to us, not so we will indulge ourselves with more stuff, but so we will spend ourselves on behalf of those in spiritual and physical need.

Let's believe that Jesus is worthy of all our desire—he is utterly satisfying, and we have no need to seek the pleasures of this world, because we have found ultimate delight in him.

Let's believe that Jesus is worthy of all our affections—he has loved us completely, so we will adore him supremely.

Let's believe that Jesus is worthy of all our lives—we will gladly lose them in this world because our eyes are fixed on the world to come.

O Christian, is Jesus worth this to you?

Notes

1. Luke 9:57–58
2. Luke 9:60
3. Luke 9:62
4. John 6:53
5. Luke 14:26
6. Luke 14:27
7. Luke 14:33
8. Luke 18:22
9. Mark 10:21, emphasis added
10. Matthew 13:44

ABOUT THE
AUTHOR

Dr. David Platt is the senior pastor of the Church at Brook Hills, Birmingham, Alabama. He and his wife, Heather, have two sons. David is the author of *Radical: Taking Back Your Faith from the American Dream* (see www.radicalthebook.com).

What is Jesus worth to you?

"David Platt challenges Christians to wake up, trade in false values rooted in the American Dream, and embrace the notion that each of us is blessed by God for a global purpose…This is a must-read for every believer!"

—*Wess Stafford,*
President and CEO,
Compassion International

Radical is a daring call for Christians to believe and obey the gospel according to Jesus—even if it flies in the face of success according to the American church. David Platt reveals what can happen when we exchange our convenient beliefs for authentic discipleship.

Find information, tools for individual application, church resources, and video at
RadicalTheBook.com.

Radical: The Bible Study

Dig deeper into the powerful truths and share them with your church, Sunday school class, or small group.

- Eight Bible Study lessons correspond to the eight book chapters of *Radical*
- Each lesson includes commentary, teaching plans, discussion questions, and more
- Designed to challenge believers to put the *Radical* concepts into practice

Order at www.lifebiblestudy.com/radical or call 877.265.1605

Brought to you by LifeBibleStudy®